JOHN R. ANDERSON | *Expanded*

73
ART AGENCY

JOHN R. ANDERSON | *Expanded*

73 Art Agency
Denver, Colorado
info@73artagency.com
www.73artagency.com

Front Cover: *404*, Acrylic on canvas (framed), 2020, 48 x 36 in (122 x 91 cm)
Back Cover: photo courtesy of Lisa Jones

ISBN 978-1-950484-49-2

Published by Spring Cedars
Denver, Colorado
www.springcedars.com

We are honored to present *Expanded*, the third catalogue of John R. Anderson's extraordinary body of work. This collection showcases 41 newly discovered paintings retrieved from the artist's studio in Yankton, South Dakota—each a testament to his lifelong commitment to exploration and reinvention.

Even in his final years, Anderson remained deeply engaged with his art, continuously evolving his approach and embracing new, creative challenges. His passion for painting never waned; he saw each canvas as an opportunity for discovery, each brushstroke as a step toward something greater. This catalogue not only highlights the latest chapter of his artistic journey but also pays tribute to the visionary spirit that defined his career.

With *Expanded*, we celebrate an artist who never ceased to push the boundaries of Lyrical Abstraction, an artist who saw creativity as an ever-unfolding process. We invite you to explore this collection and experience the vibrancy, energy, and depth that continue to make Anderson's work both compelling and timeless.

We extend our deepest gratitude to all who contributed to this exhibition and publication. A special thanks to Christine Anderson, whose dedication has been invaluable in bringing this project to life.

73 Art Agency

"Through the 2020 South Dakota Art Museum exhibition *Abstraction: Eight South Dakotans* (curated by Jodi Lundgren), our staff had the pleasure of working with John R. Anderson and his wife, Christine. Viewing rows of Anderson's canvases—poured, brushed, and scraped with a remarkable sense of balance, intuition, and accident—was a memorable experience, set against the sweeping Yankton, South Dakota landscape beyond their home.

As the oldest artist in the exhibition, Anderson brought valuable historical perspective to Abstract art movements from the 1950s onward. His recent works, created more than sixty years into his career and selected for the show, were as fresh and compelling as ever. We were honored by his decision to donate the painting *Dakota Modern* to the museum's permanent collection, where it now resides in conversation with works by South Dakota abstract contemporaries Signe Stuart, Alice Berry, and John E. Anderson."

~ Taylor McKeown, Collections & Exhibitions Curator, South Dakota Art Museum

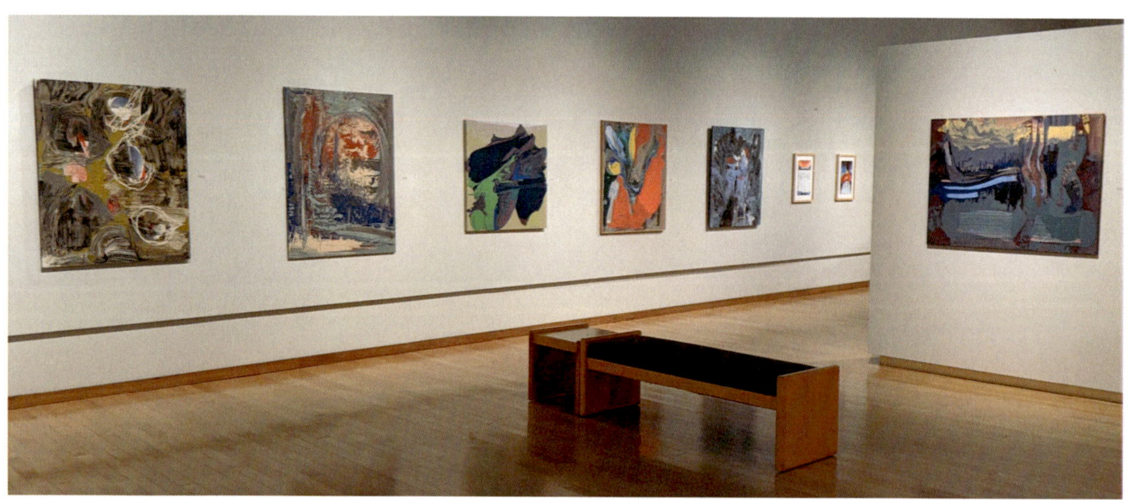

ABSTRACTION: Eight South Dakotans gallery shot, South Dakota, 2020, courtesy of South Dakota Art Museum

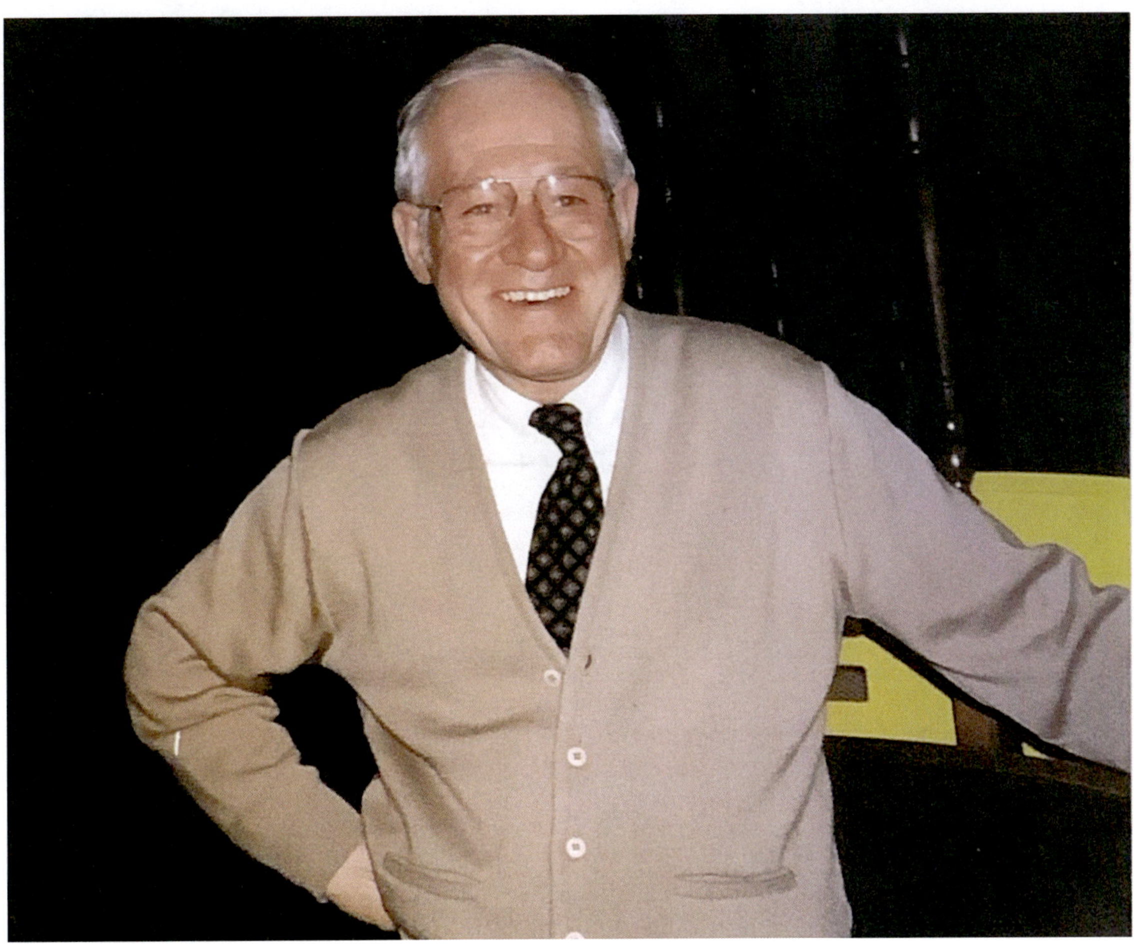

Anderson, 1993, courtesy of Christine Anderson

"I discovered Anderson's paintings late. He is not in the history books on modern art, not in the big and expensive New York galleries, never made the cover of *Time* magazine, did not lose his mind. Yet every one of his paintings is at least interesting, many excellent. He does not repeat himself because this particular style sells well or is trendy, instead each painting is the result of an independent research and inhabits its own universe.

I like that he was able to follow his personal path unencumbered and not be stuck in one corner, reinventing style when needed. I find his sense of shape and color very creative and original, and he knows how to start and when to stop a painting. I liken his approach to that of a medieval artisan who honestly produces work with all their ability, creating what we call art almost without knowing it. To me he is one of these artists that posterity will recognize as more important than their time."

~ Frederick Pichon, Artist, M. Arch. École Nationale Supérieure d'Architecture de Paris-Belleville, France

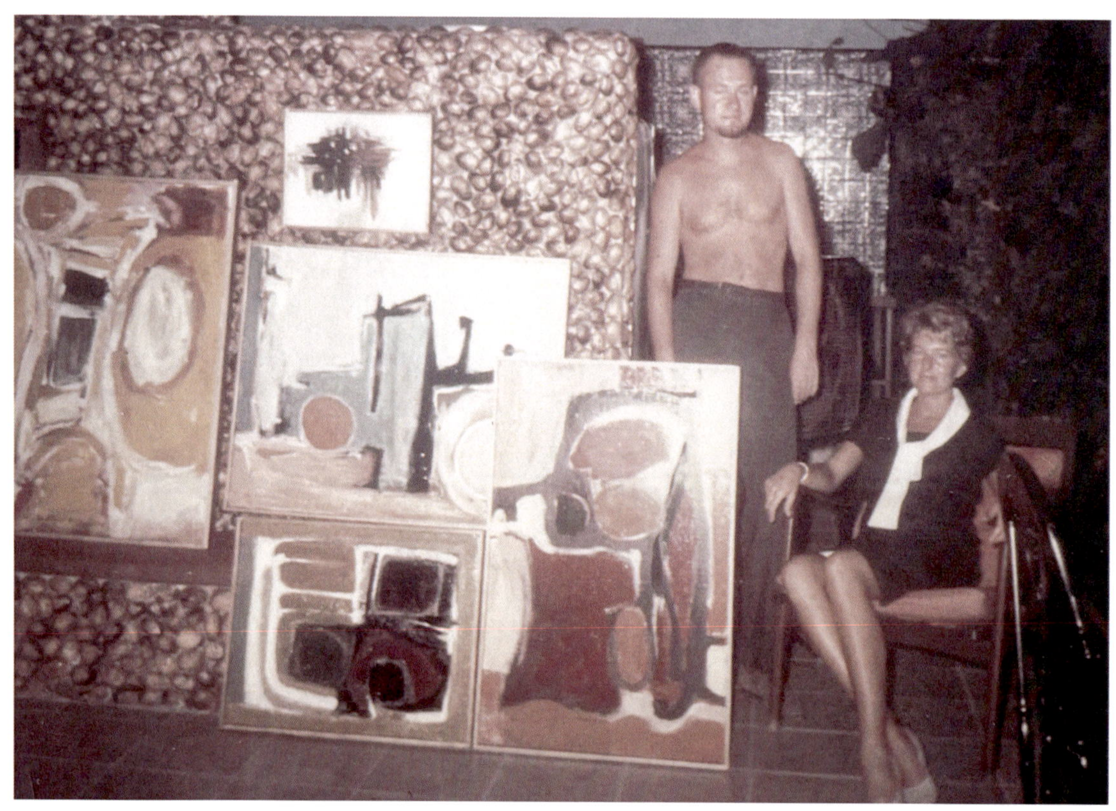

Anderson with wife Christine, Mazatlán, 1965, courtesy of Christine Anderson

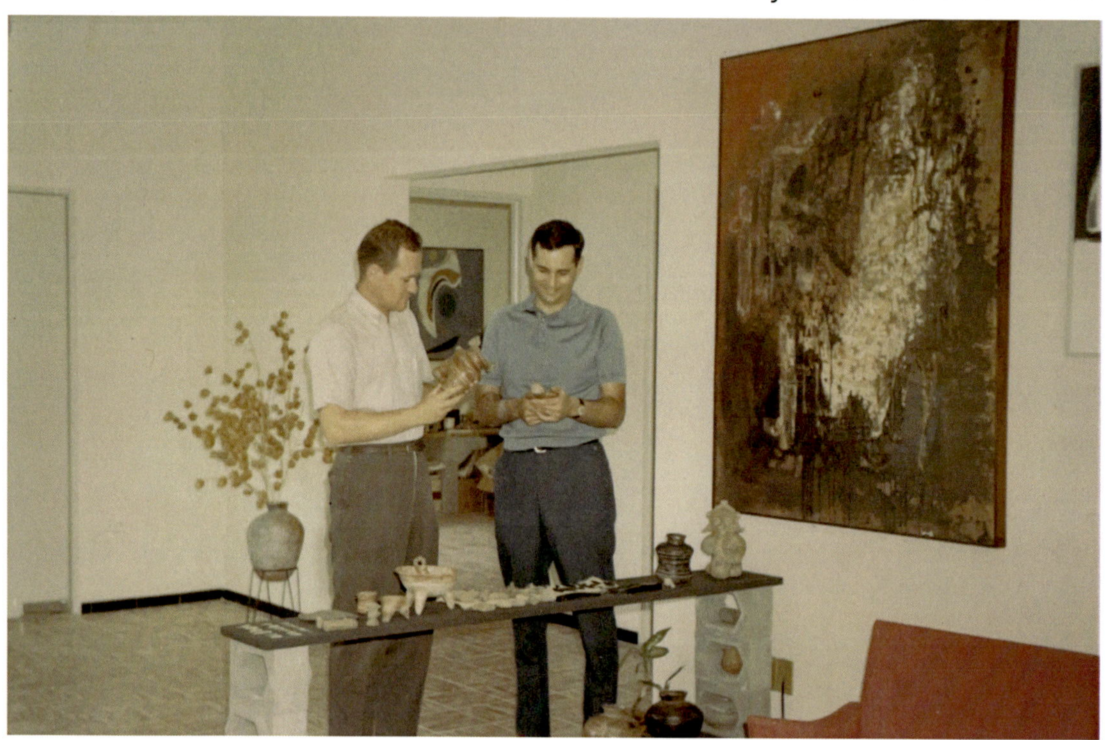

Anderson (left) with friend, Guadalajara, 1967, courtesy of Christine Anderson

JOHN R. ANDERSON: INFINITE CREATIVE GROWTH

At the age of 90, abstract artist John R. Anderson still had a boyish enthusiasm for his work, often painting into the small hours of the morning. He expanded creatively, pleased to still be stretching his limits, yet always deeply serious and ambitious with his art.

The world of art lost a visionary when John R. Anderson passed away on December 6, 2021. He leaves behind a legacy that continues to inspire and captivate. His relentless pursuit of artistic evolution and unwavering passion for his craft remained intact. This third catalogue *Expanded* unveils 41 new paintings retrieved from his studio in Yankton, South Dakota, making evident that Anderson's creative journey knew no bounds.

Artists might slow down or rest on their laurels in their twilight years, but John R. Anderson was different. He embraced each day as an opportunity to explore new techniques and unearth hidden dimensions within his art. To him, painting was not just a passion; it was a lifelong adventure, a means to discover the uncharted territories of creativity.

Anderson's work is representative of the Lyrical Abstraction style of the 1960s, a grand melody of color, texture, and movement. He approaches the canvas with expressive brushstrokes and emphasizes the physical act of painting as an essential part of the finished product. What goes on the canvas is not a picture, but an event. The gesture on the canvas is one of liberation.

In his eighties, the artist continued to paint lyrical abstractions akin to the works included in his two previous collections *Uncovered* and *Explored*, i.e., with flow, brush, simplification, and shaping. He also ventured in other stylistic directions—an experiment which the artist equated in and of itself with success. "Seeing more and more" as he aged, Anderson's art evolved in tandem with his experiences and perceptions of the world.

In terms of technique, Anderson's latest and last artistic pursuit incorporates more splatter than flow. Anderson selected a uniform size of canvas, relatively smaller than the dimensions of previous works. "It's not that big, but it's got the power. I like it because there's a new approach that was successful, and that can happen on a smaller painting and also a larger painting." (Anderson, May 2021) *Expanded* reflects a constant progression based on experiences that allow for greater freedom. The artwork is pulsating with life.

"You have to realize that my job is to build and to make sensible decisions over the progress. I strive for something, and then I come up with something a little more inventive, a new approach. Well, naturally, I zero in on that, and I'm appreciative of that effort. Whereas with some of the older ones, they're kind of tried and true. Being an artist, I'm always trying to get a new look." (Anderson, May 2021)

Expanded bears witness to this unwavering commitment to artistic growth. The name is a fitting tribute to the ever-expanding horizons of John R. Anderson's creativity. The sheer brilliance of Anderson's artistic evolution lay in his ability to hold on to the core tenets of his lyrical abstract style while pushing the boundaries of expression. His masterful use of the brush, both for simplification and shaping, reveal the hand of a seasoned artist who knew precisely where to wield each stroke.

His works speak of a profound understanding of colors, shapes, and emotions. In each mark, with every layer of paint, one can witness the passion, the joy, and the unyielding ambition that fueled his artistic journey. His determination to evolve and defy the constraints of time profoundly impacts those who encounter his works.

As we contemplate these 41 new paintings, we find ourselves in awe of an artist who remained ageless and embraced each moment with the fervor of a newcomer and the wisdom of a master. John R. Anderson's artistic odyssey is a testament to the boundless nature of creativity, an enduring reminder that true art knows no age and that the human spirit can eternally strive for new frontiers of expression. His art will continue to resonate with generations to come.

"I think that I am improving and if I had the slightest doubt, then I would not do this. What we are looking at now is on a different level. I believe it's going to happen. It makes me happy thinking about it." (Anderson, September 2021)

John R. Anderson was born in Yankton, South Dakota, in 1931. He attended the University of South Dakota and the Minneapolis School of Fine Arts, where he participated in Oskar Kokoschka's 1952 symposia. He earned his Bachelor of Fine Art at the University of Denver School of Art in 1958, when Vance Kirkland was its director. Anderson and his wife, Christine Sheail, then moved to Mexico for three years where he painted extensively and held his first major show at the Guadalajara Jalisco State Gallery. He also showed his work in Dallas and subsequently resided in London and Denver prior to his return to Yankton.

Anderson painted at the forefront of the Lyrical Abstraction movement. His first catalogue *Uncovered* reviews the historical context of lyrical abstract art, and the second catalogue *Explored* analyzes the artist's technique and process.

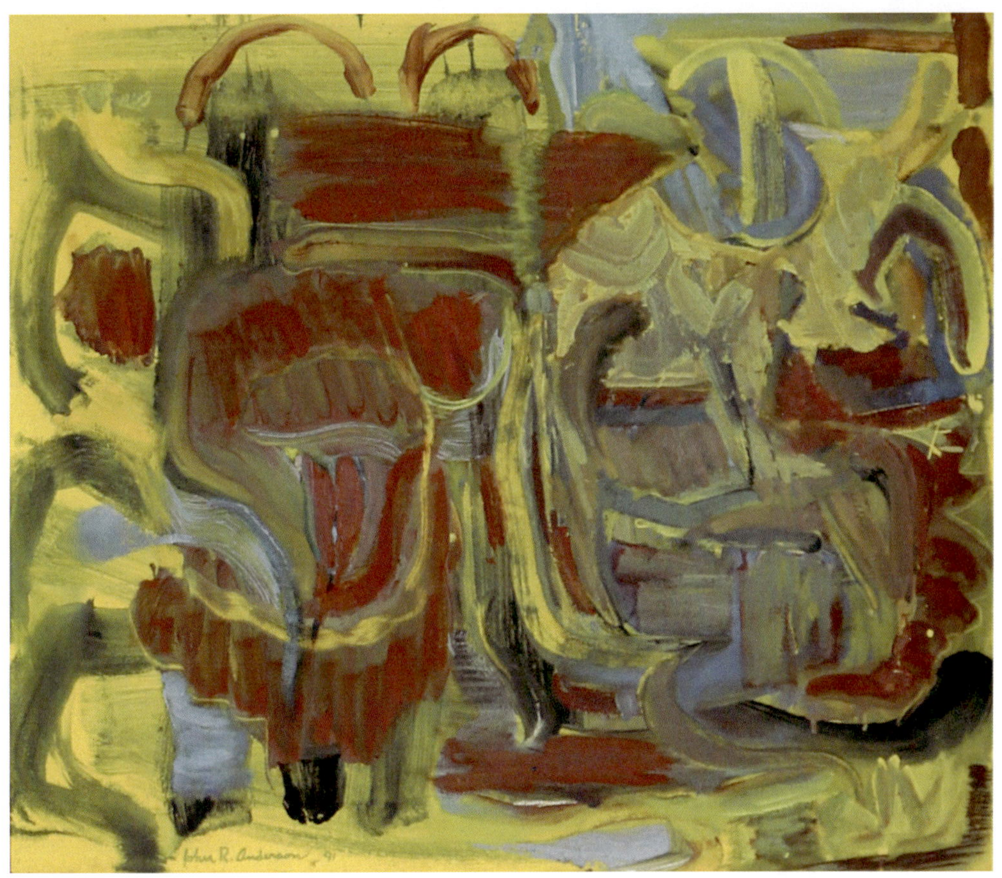

79
Acrylic on canvas (framed)
1997
29.75 x 34.5 in (76 x 88 cm)

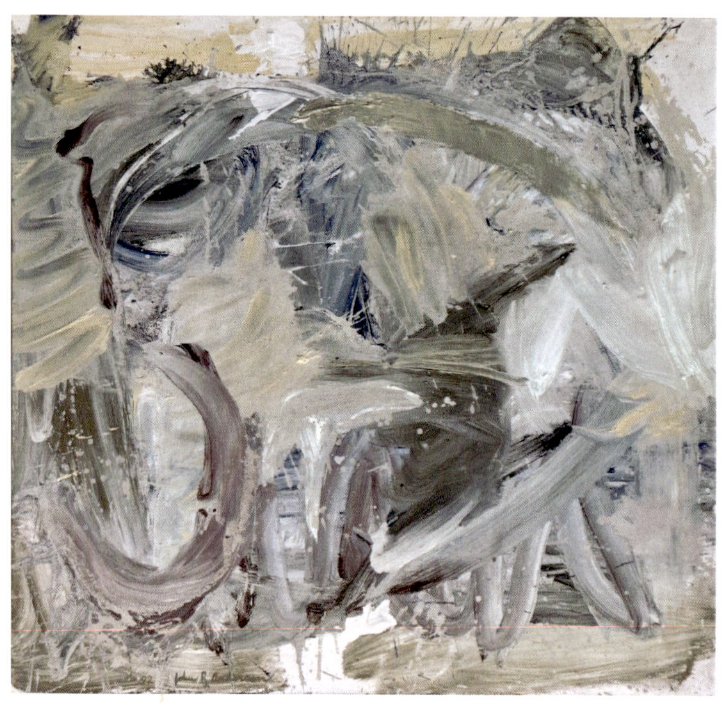

144
Acrylic on canvas (framed)
1992
40 x 43 in (102 x 109 cm)

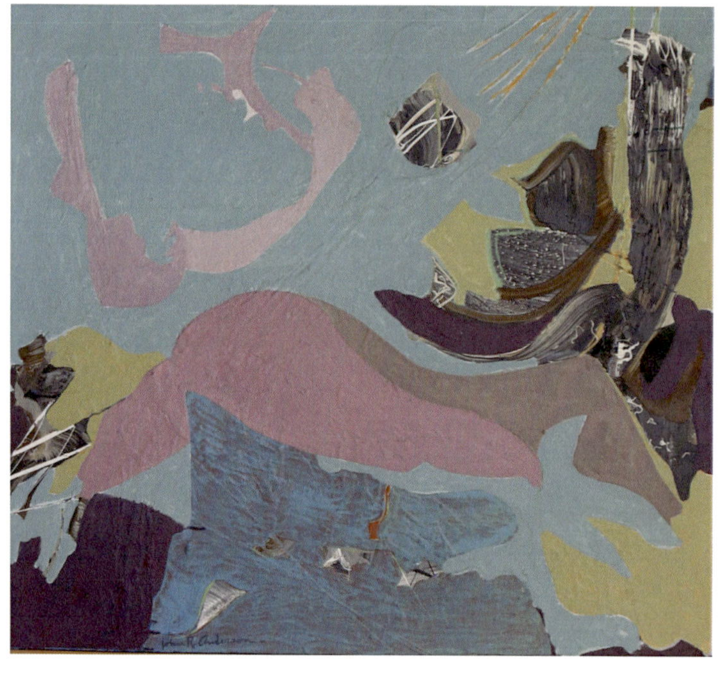

185
Acrylic on canvas (framed)
2008–2021
34 x 38 in (86 x 97 cm)

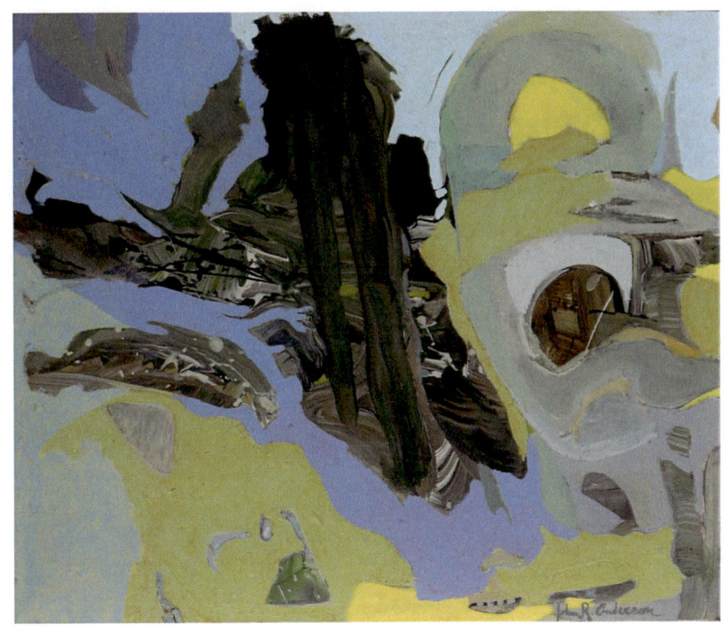

189
Acrylic on canvas (framed)
2002–2017
24 x 29 in (61 x 74 cm)

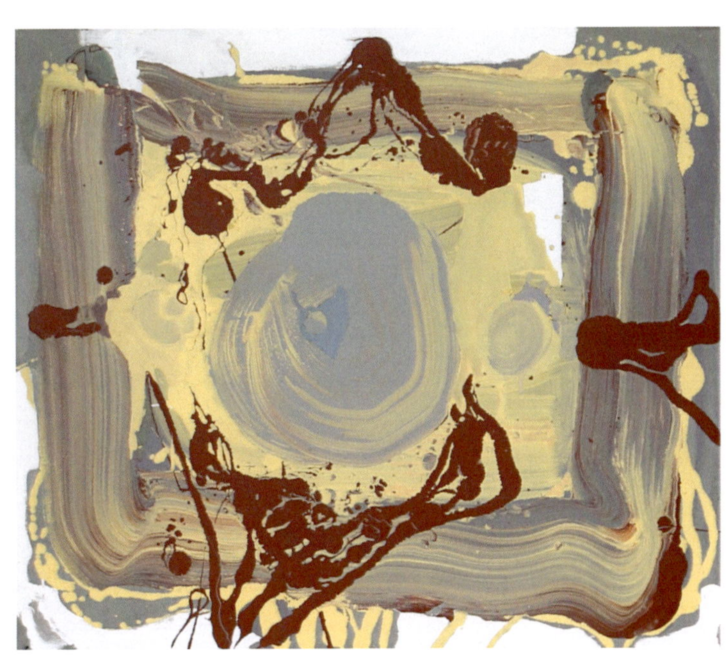

198
Acrylic on canvas
2008
24 x 28 in (61 x 71 cm)

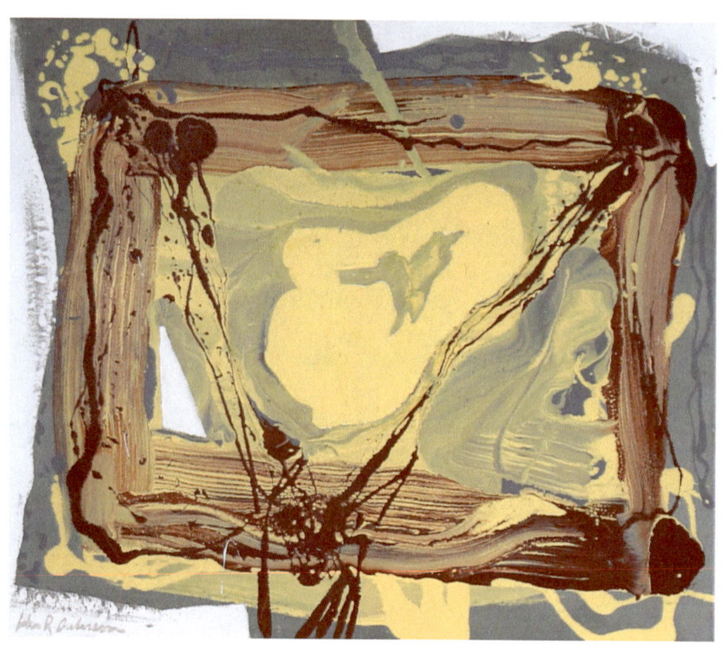

199
Acrylic on canvas
2008
24 x 28 in (61 x 71 cm)

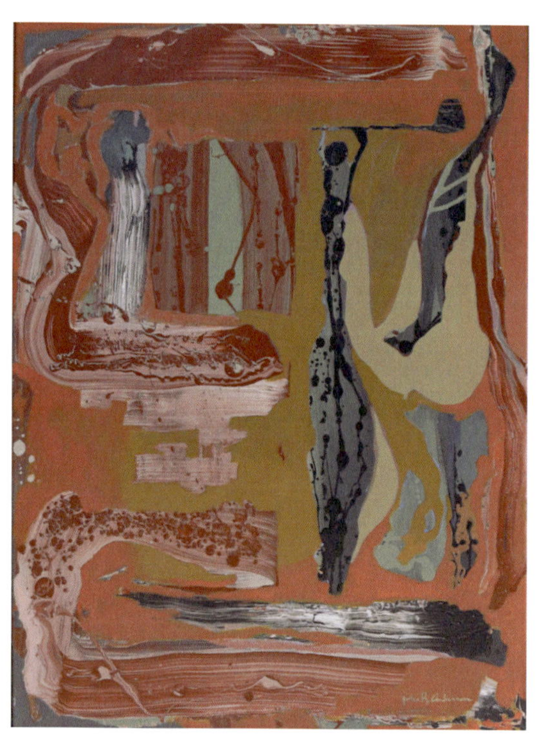

213
Acrylic on canvas
2008–2020
40 x 30 in (102 x 76 cm)

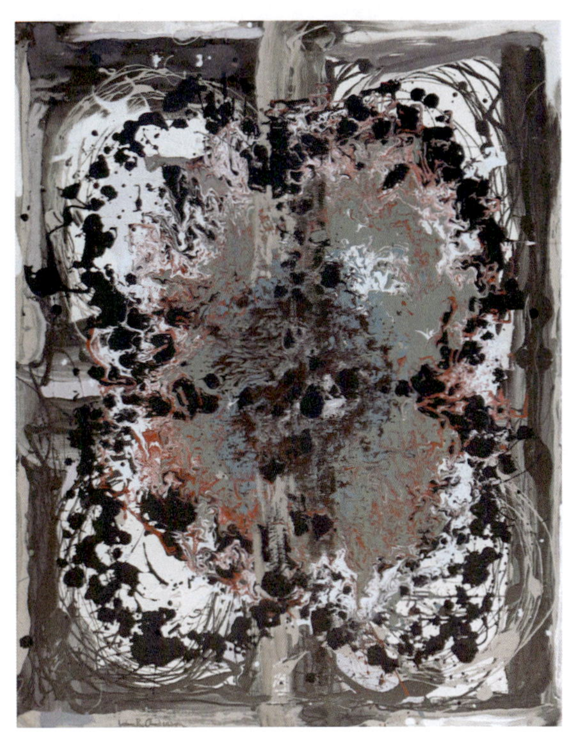

224
Acrylic on canvas (framed)
2008–2018
45 x 36 in (114 x 91 cm)

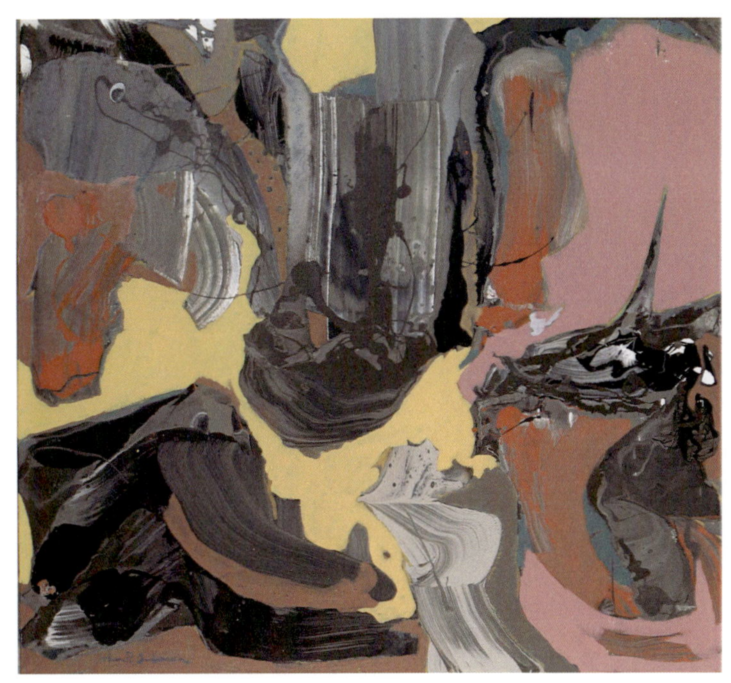

225
Acrylic on canvas
2008–2012
32 x 35.5 in (81 x 90 cm)

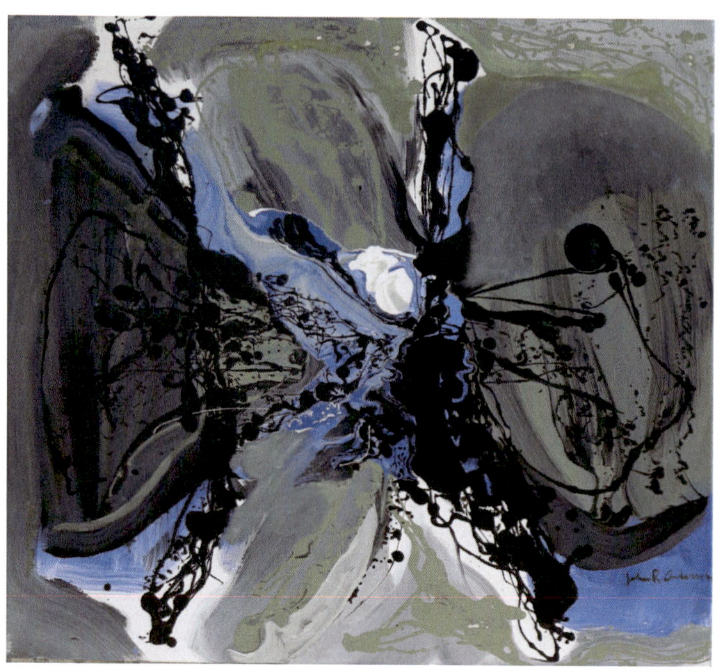

230
Acrylic on canvas
2008–2012
36 x 41 in (91 x 104 cm)

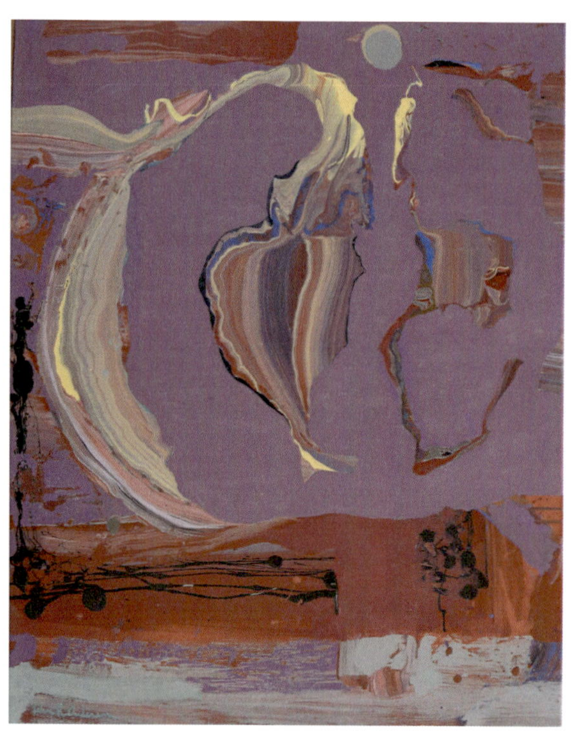

232
Acrylic on canvas (framed)
2008–2020
46 x 38 in (117 x 97 cm)

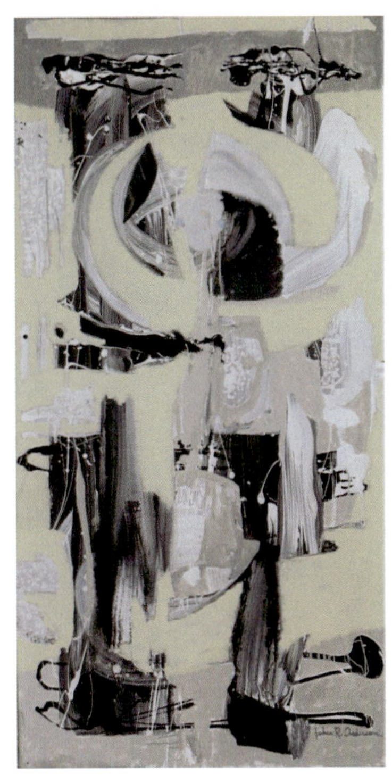

236
Acrylic on canvas
2009–2020
51 x 26 in (130 x 66 cm)

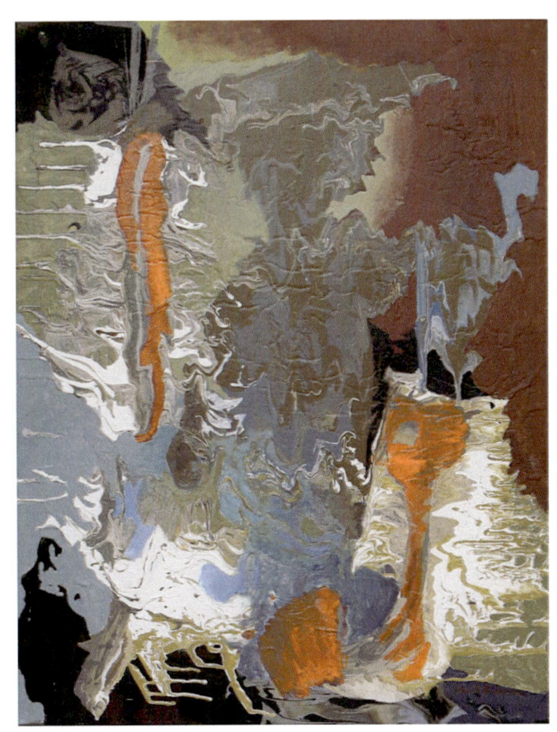

243
Acrylic on canvas
1999–2012
40.5 x 32 in (103 x 81 cm)

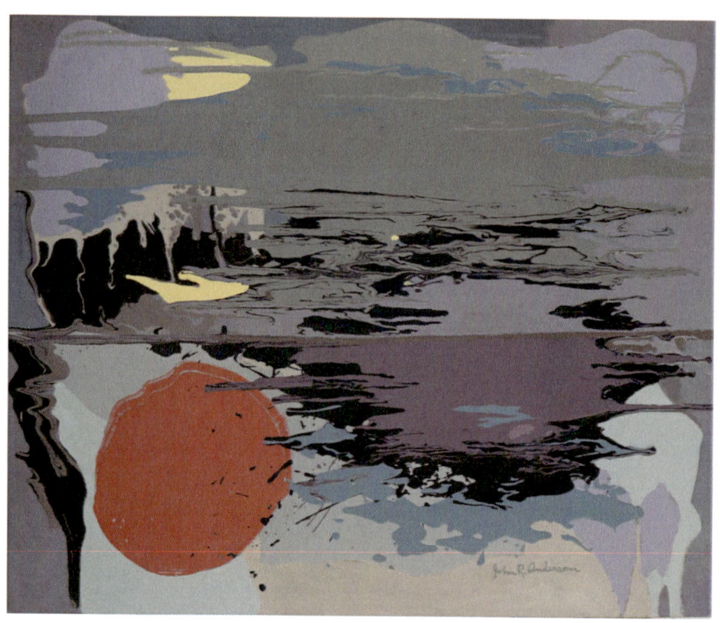

246
Acrylic on canvas
1999–2019
35.5 x 43 in (90 x 109 cm)

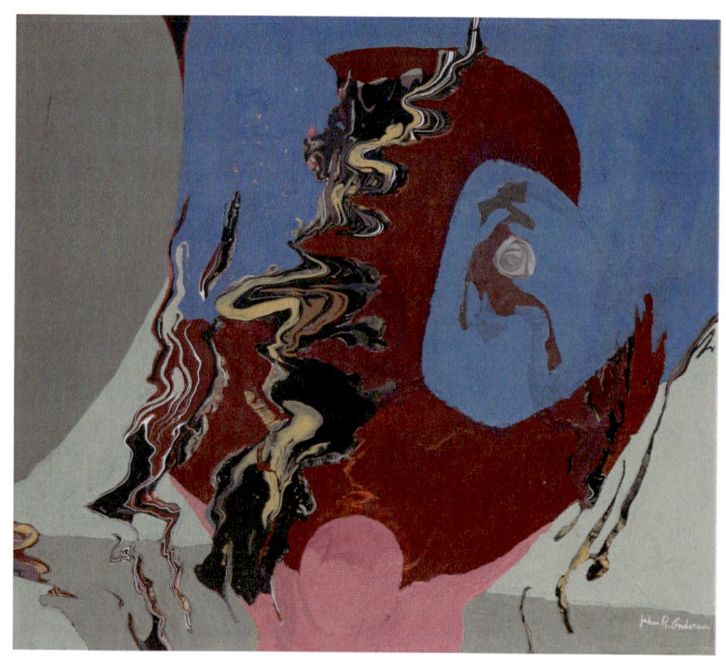

257
Acrylic on canvas (framed)
2009–2017
30 x 35 in (76 x 89 cm)

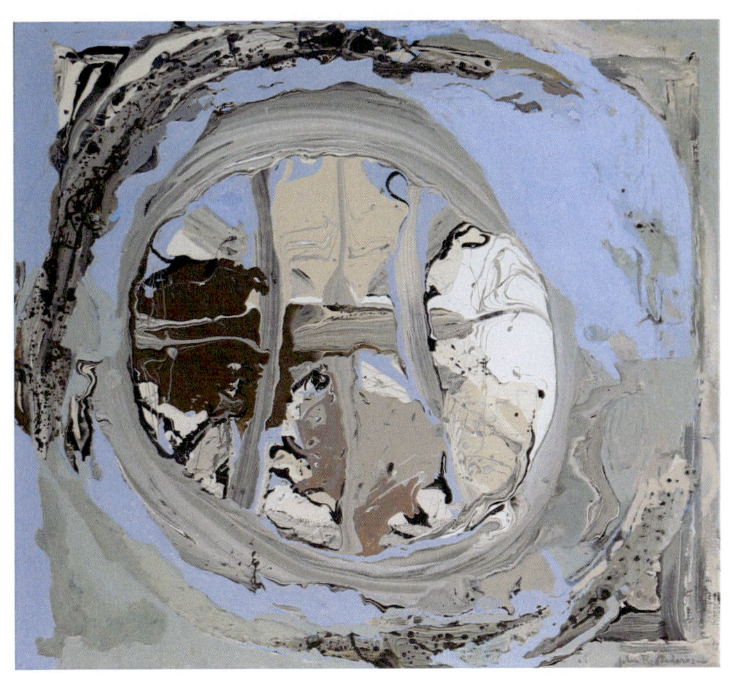

282
Acrylic on canvas (framed)
1991–2016
30 x 34 in (76 x 86 cm)

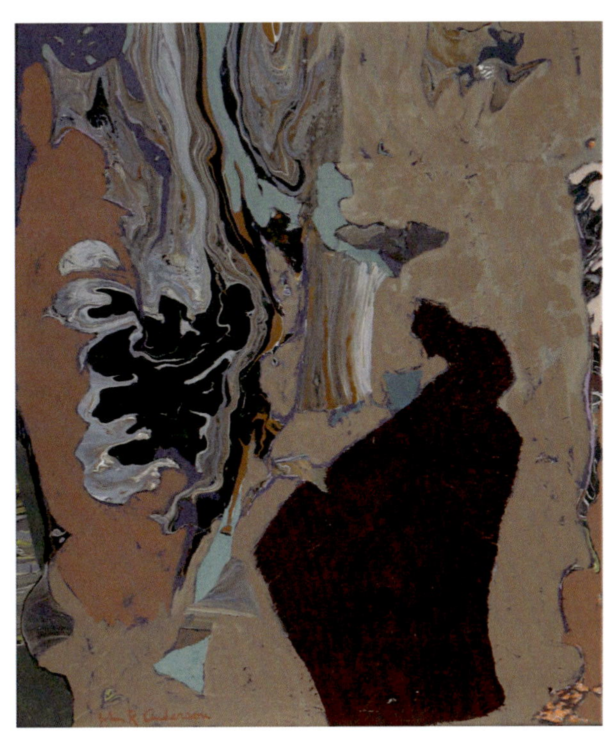

284
Acrylic on canvas (framed)
2009–2021
34 x 29 in (86 x 74 cm)

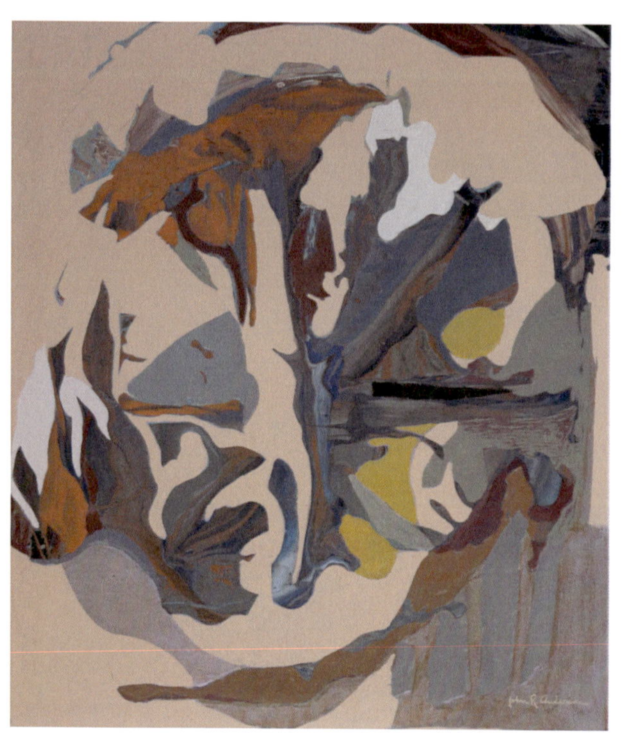

300
Acrylic on canvas (framed)
2007–2020
41 x 36 in (104 x 91 cm)

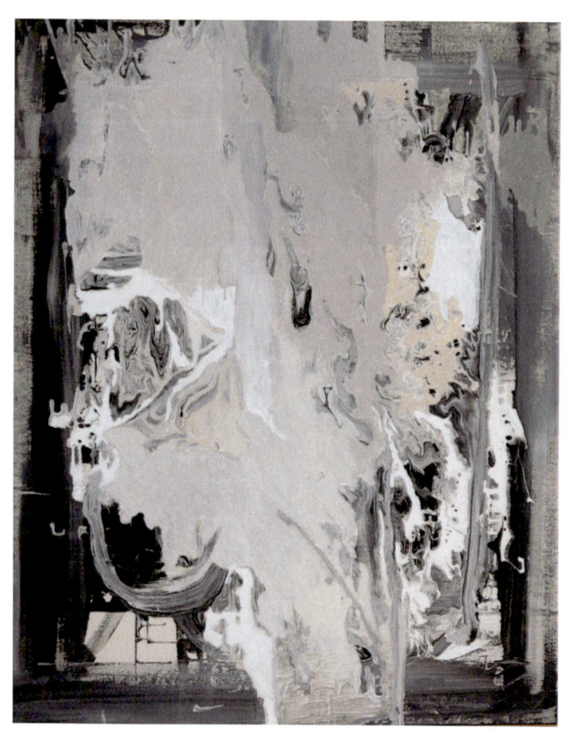

306
Acrylic on canvas (framed)
2010–2018
42 x 34 in (107 x 86 cm)

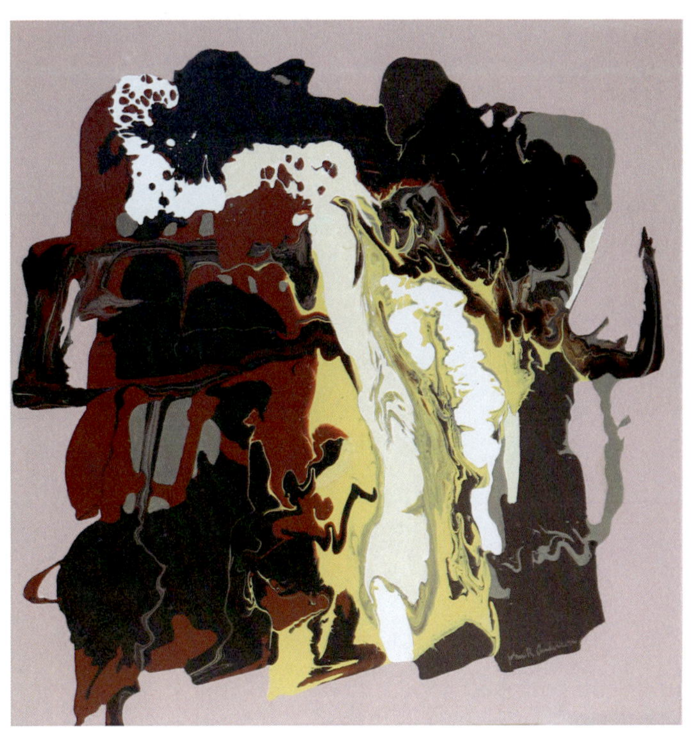

323
Acrylic on canvas
2013–2018
40 x 40 in (102 x 102 cm)

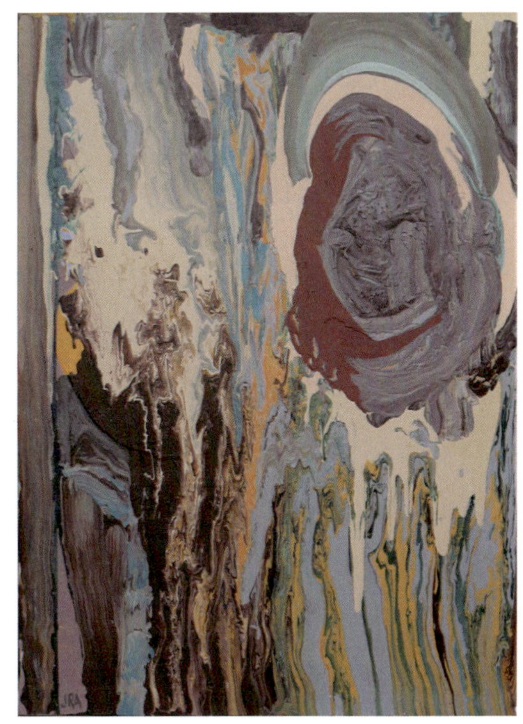

349
Acrylic on canvas
2018
40 x 30 in (102 x 76 cm)

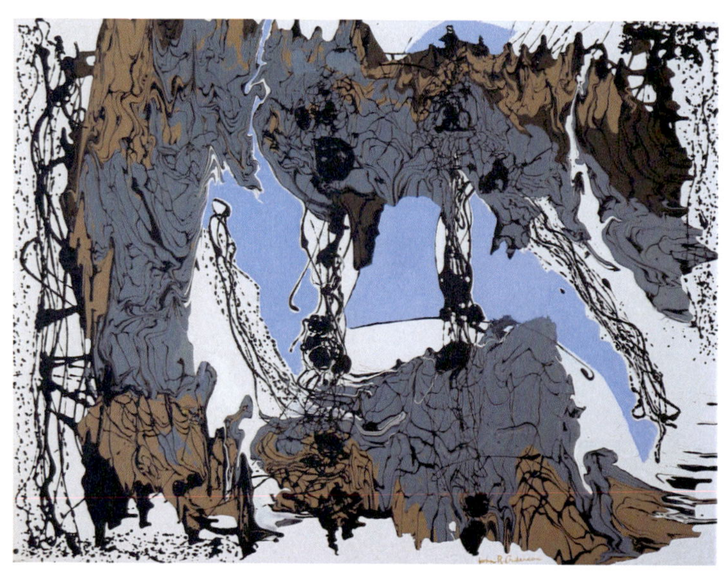

357
Acrylic on canvas (framed)
2019
36 x 48 in (91 x 122 cm)

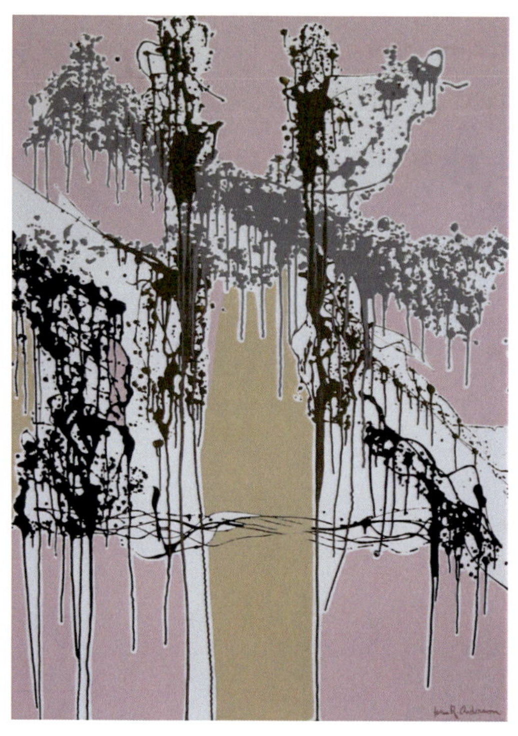

360
Acrylic on canvas (framed)
2019
48 x 36 in (122 x 91 cm)

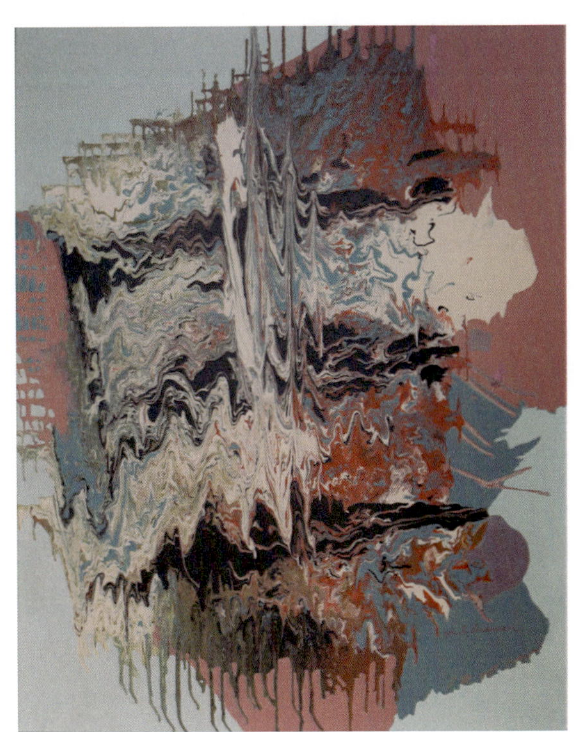

364
Acrylic on canvas
2019
50 x 40 in (127 x 102 cm)

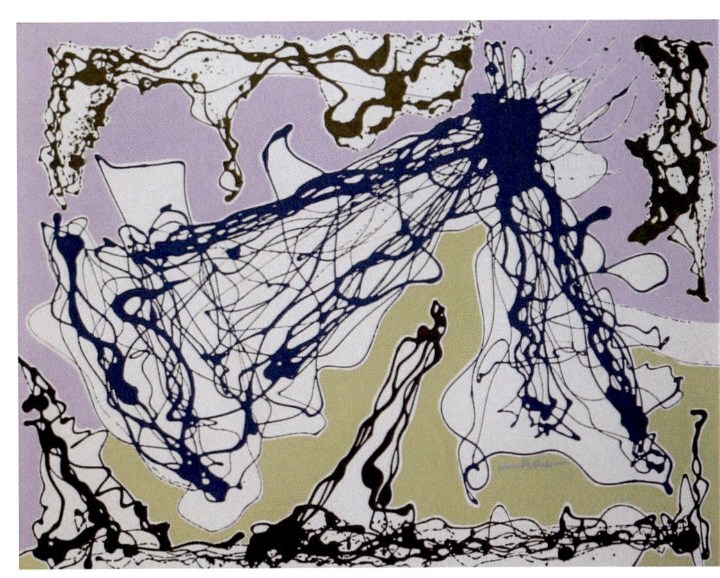

372
Acrylic on canvas (framed)
2019
36 x 48 in (91 x 122 cm)

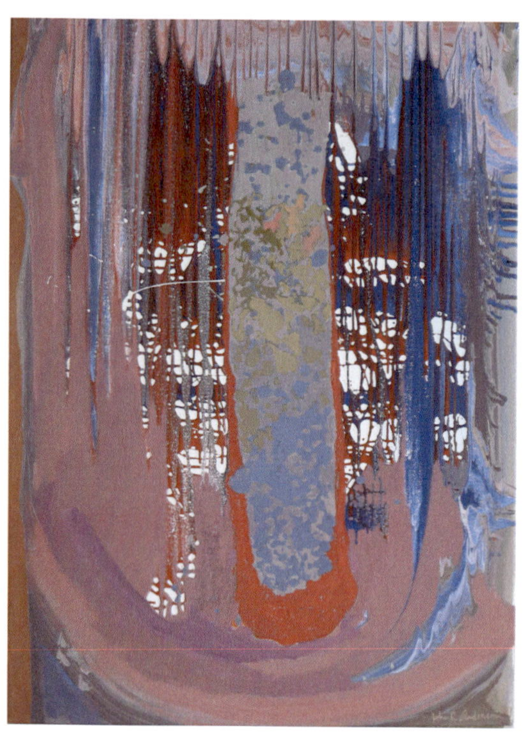

377
Acrylic on canvas
2018–2021
48 x 36 in (122 x 91 cm)

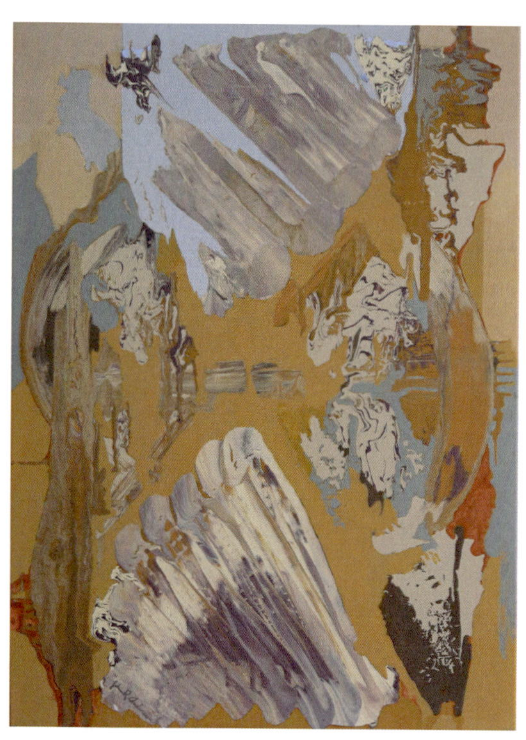

388
Acrylic on canvas (framed)
2019
48 x 36 in (122 x 91 cm)

393
Acrylic on canvas (framed)
2020
36 x 48 in (91 x 122 cm)

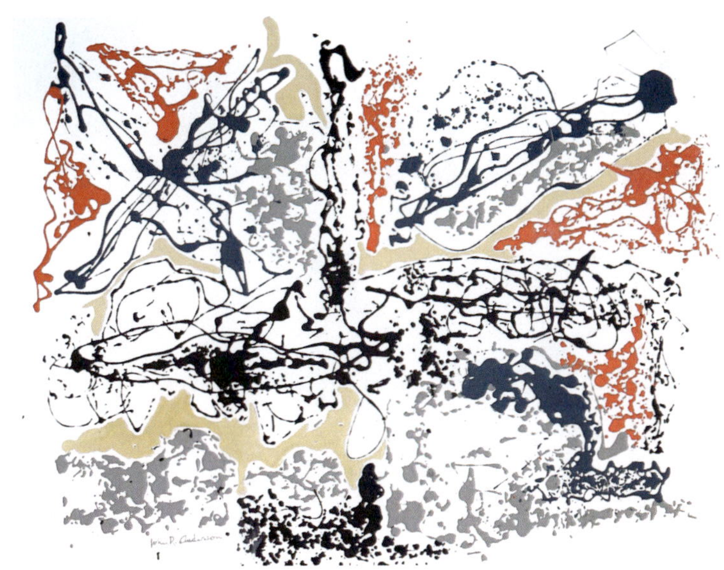

398
Acrylic on canvas (framed)
2020
48 x 36 in (122 x 91 cm)

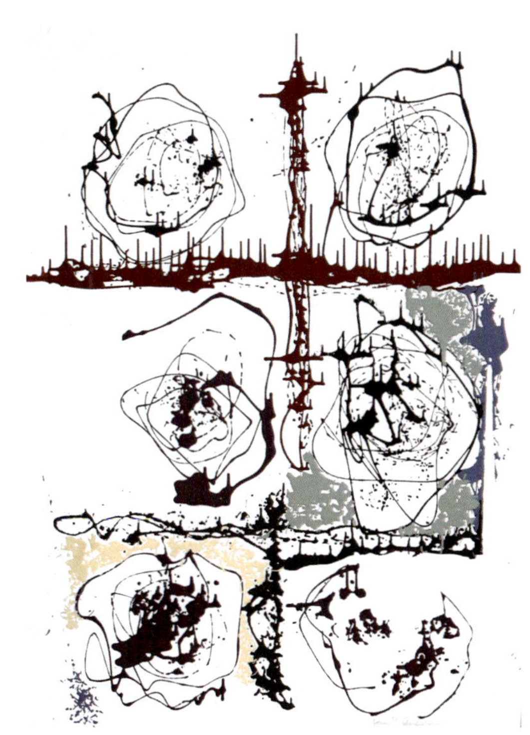

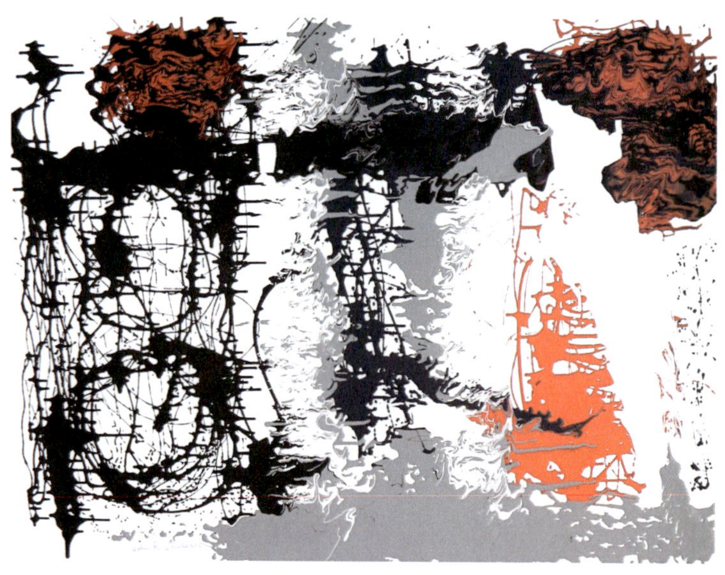

403
Acrylic on canvas (framed)
2020
36 x 48 in (91 x 122 cm)

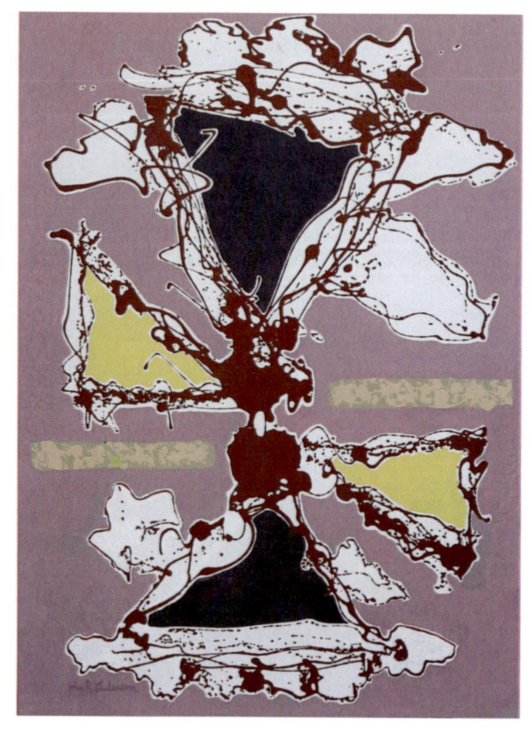

404
Acrylic on canvas (framed)
2020
48 x 36 in (122 x 91 cm)

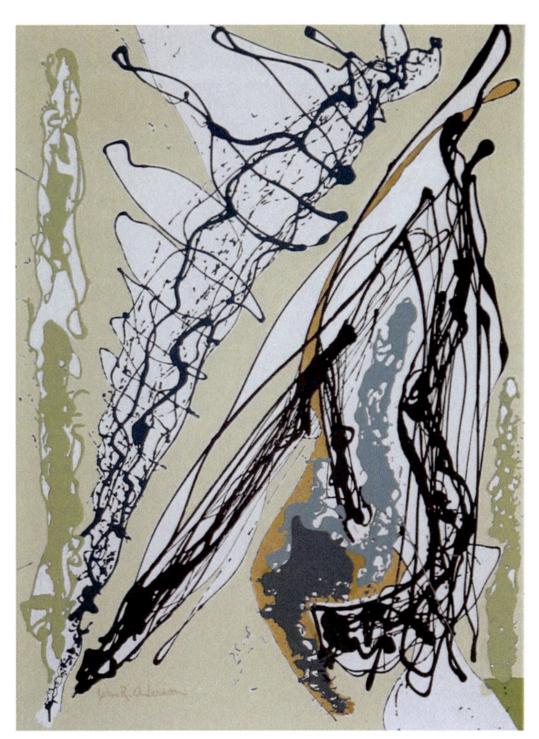

405
Acrylic on canvas (framed)
2020
48 x 36 in (122 x 91 cm)

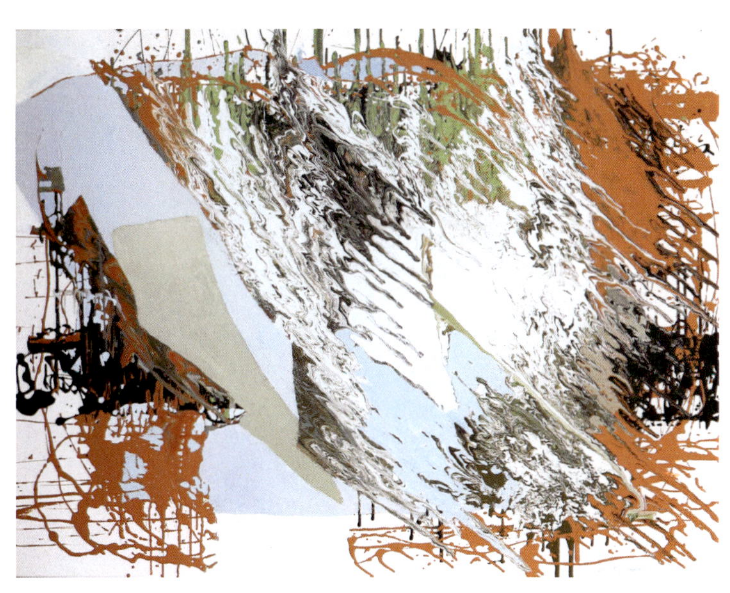

406
Acrylic on canvas (framed)
2020–2021
36 x 48 in (91 x 122 cm)

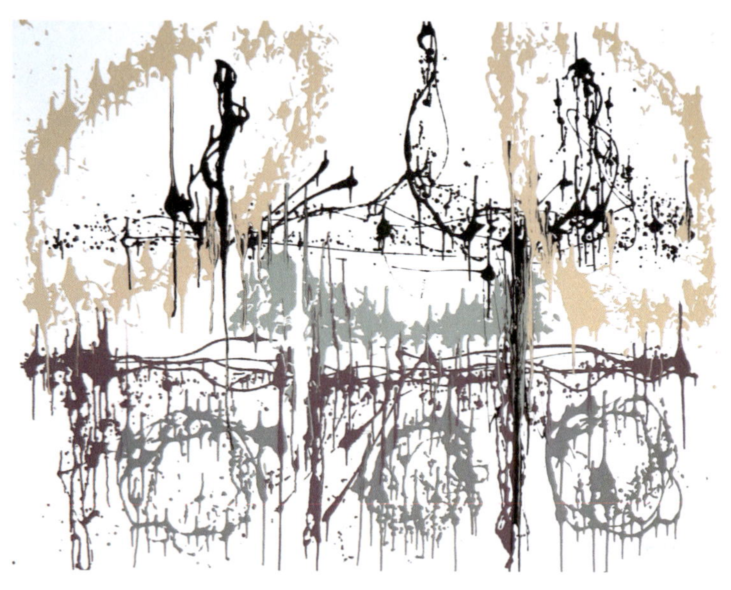

408
Acrylic on canvas (framed)
2020
36 x 48 in (91 x 122 cm)

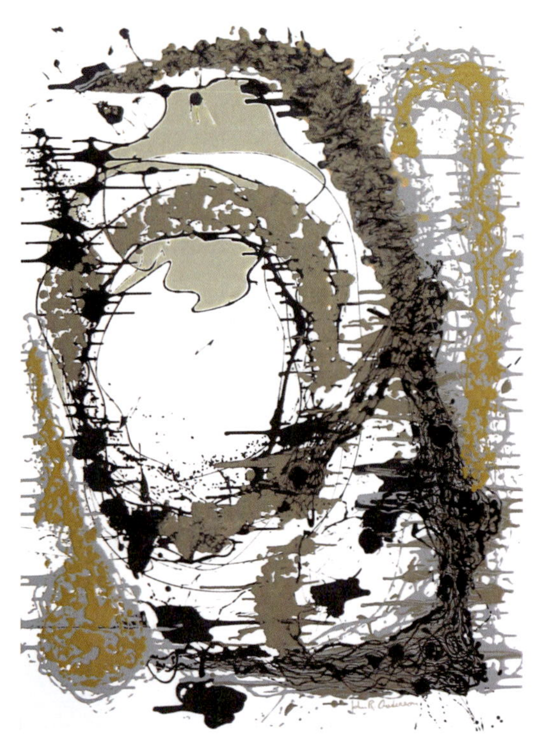

411
Acrylic on canvas (framed)
2020
48 x 36 in (122 x 91 cm)

415
Acrylic on canvas (framed)
2021
36 x 48 in (91 x 122 cm)

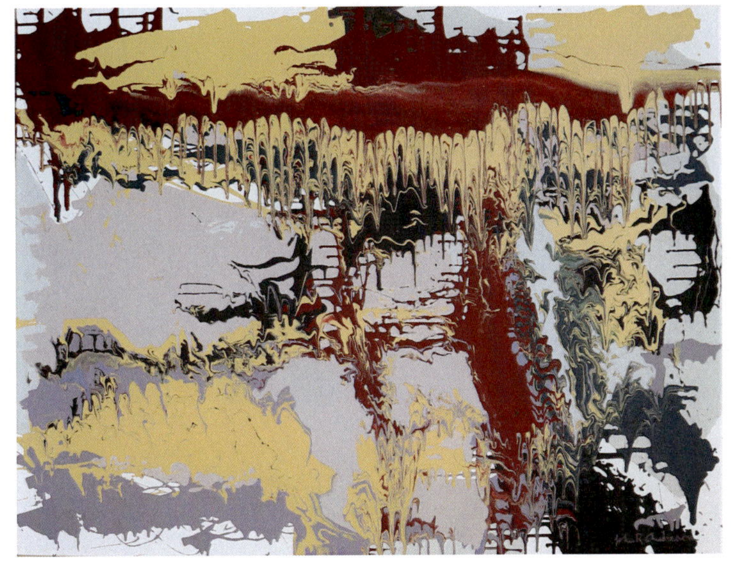

417
Acrylic on canvas (framed)
2021
48 x 36 in (122 x 91 cm)

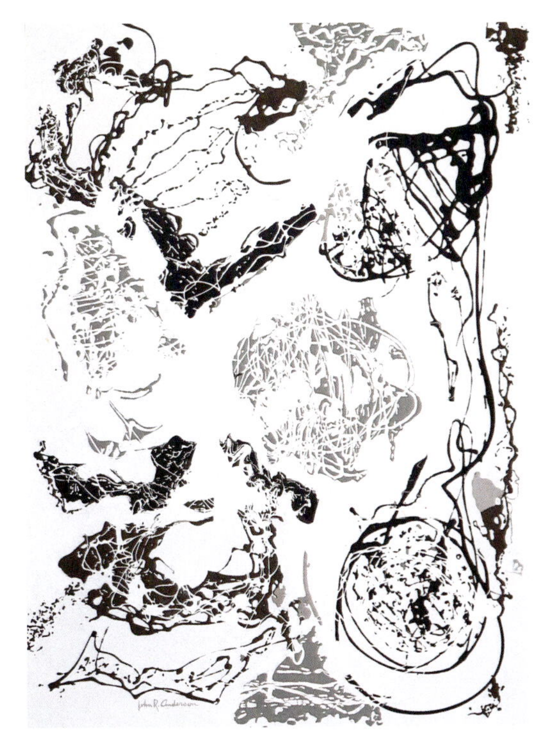

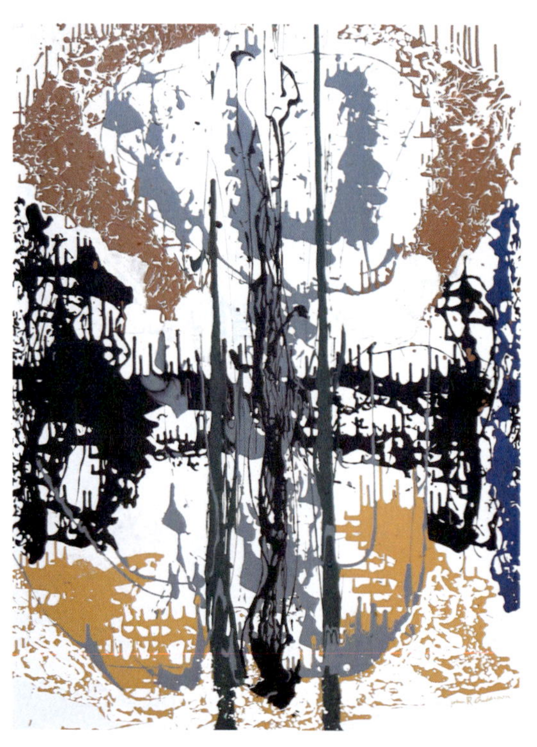

422
Acrylic on canvas (framed)
2021
48 x 36 in (122 x 91 cm)

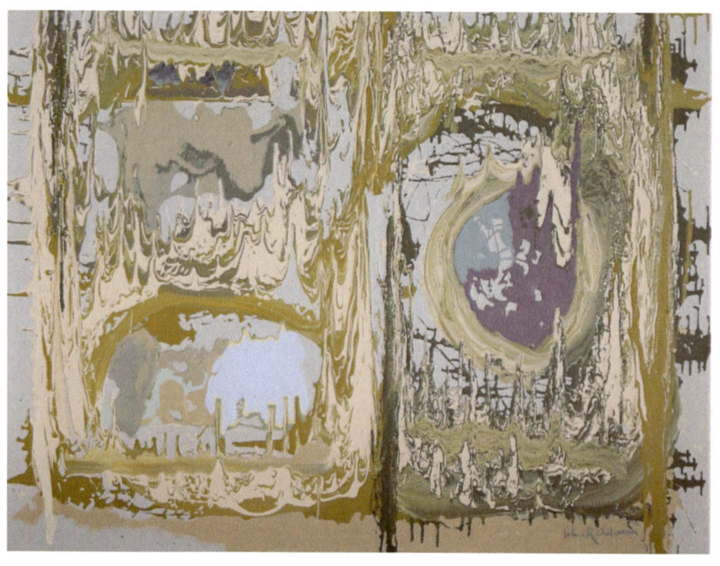

423
Acrylic on canvas (framed)
2021
36 x 48 in (91 x 122 cm)

431
Acrylic on canvas (framed)
2021
48 x 36 in (122 x 91 cm)

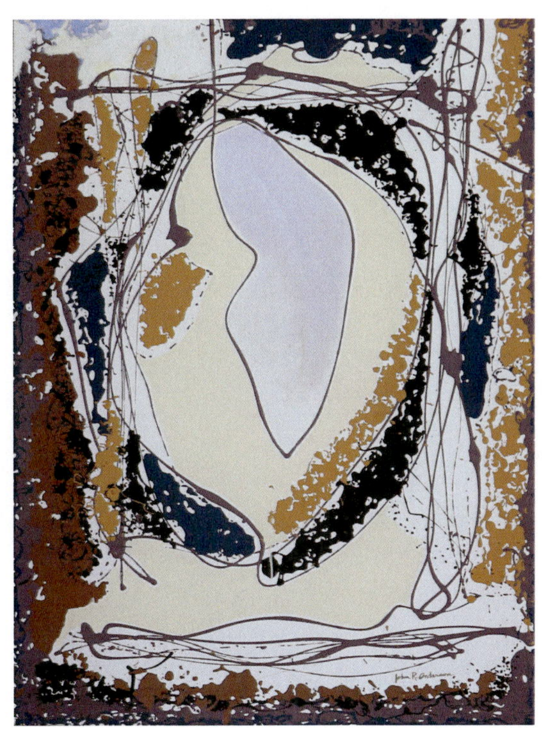

432
Acrylic on canvas (framed)
2021
48 x 36 in (122 x 91 cm)

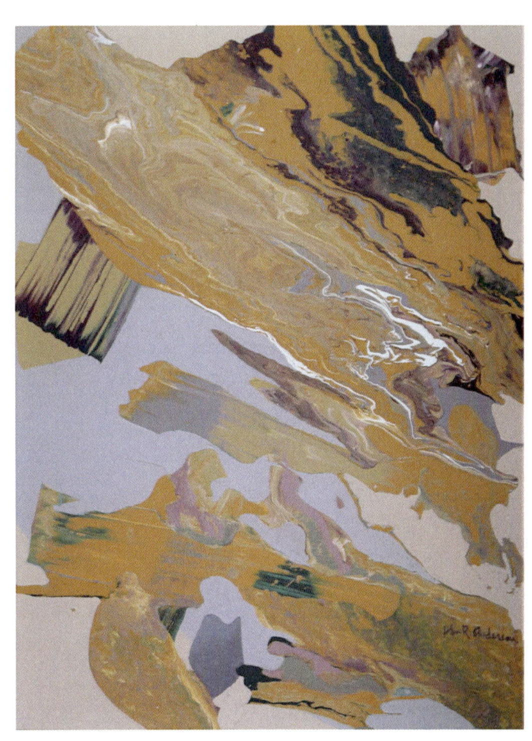

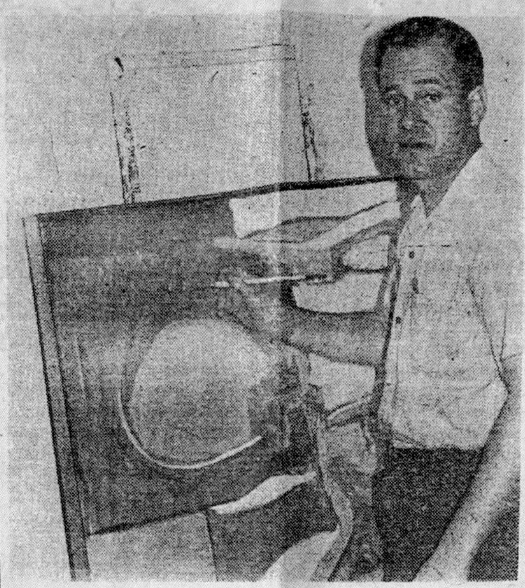

U. S. Artist Will Show At Casa de la Cultura

Slated for a one-man, March showing at the Casa de la Cultura here is an American Westerner who has been painting in México for the past year and one-half and is now a resident of Guadalajara.

He is John "Dick" Anderson, 35, who with his London-born wife, Christine, makes his home at No. 136 Circunvalación Norte in Las Fuentes.

Anderson, a native of South Dakota, has been painting since he attended the Minneapolis School of Art and later the University of Denver where he finished his formal training in 1958, and almost from the beginning it has been abstract forms of expression that have attracted him.

"Before I studied," he recalls, "it had always been the realism of the Dutch masters that had appealed to me. Then I began to see that painting can express feelings and emotions as well as represent figures".

Anderson's large canvases—some of them textured with molded, plastic resin glue—have the masses of color set against great spaces that one would naturally assume to come from a background of Western prairies and planes, and although he worked for a year in Mazatlán before coming here, it is only in his recent paintings that one sees a definite "Mexican" atmosphere.

"I'm in no hurry," the husky, blue-eyed artist explains. "One thing wrong with U.S. art is that there are so many amateurs and too many young students exhibiting in América. Art takes time and concentration to mature".

Anderson has taken time out from his art for a stretch in the Army where he says he had lots of time to read when he wasn't doing caricatures. He and his attractive wife had planned to spend only a year in Guadalajara and then move down to Oaxaca, but they like it here so well they have decided to remain.

He has a hobby interest in pre-columbian ceramics and is enthusiastic over the regional arts and crafts he has found here.

Here-to-fore he has exhibited only in group shows—in the Western Annual and Metropolitan, both in Denver, and his work is now hung in the Contemporary gallery in Dallas.

His show here at the Casa will open March 6.

U. S. Artist John Anderson who will have a one-man showing of his abstractions in the Casa de la Cultura next month.

Anderson featured in *The Colony Reporter Journal*, 1967, courtesy of The Guadalajara Reporter

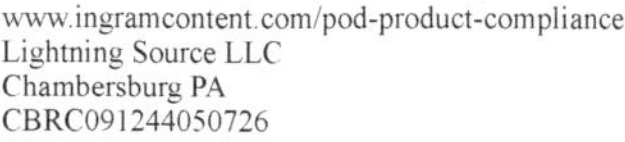